Laughs in Layers

200 Jokes for Painting Contractors

by Jeff Lockwood

Publisher – Painting Biz Publishing

ISBN: 9798298619646

Table of Contents

Dedication

To all the hardworking painting contractors—past, present, and future.

Your steady hands, long hours, and endless determination bring color and life to the world around us. May this book bring you laughter between coats and remind you that behind every brushstroke is a craftsman worth celebrating.

Best of luck,

Jeff Lockwood

Pro Painter / Author/ Painting Business Coach
    jeff@paintingbizcoach.com

Chapter 1: Brush Strokes of Humor

Every masterpiece starts with a brushstroke... and a laugh helps keep the paint from drying too slowly. On with the jokes-

Why don't painters ever get lost? Because they always stay within the lines.

I told my painter friend a joke... but he just brushed it off.

What's a painter's favorite exercise? The 9 inch roll.

Why was the painter always calm? He knew how to keep his composure.

My painter friend is colorblind... he just takes things one shade at a time.

Painting contractors don't get stressed... they just roll with it.

What did the wall say to the painter? "You crack me up!"

Why was the painter such a good musician?
He had great strokes.

My painter quit his job today… he said he
just couldn't handle the pressure.

Painting contractors are great at parties—
they always bring the rockin' roller.

**Lucas isn't spoiled . . .
but at least he's well fed.**

Chapter 2: Jobsite Humor

A homeowner asked if I could paint her ceiling "cloud white." So, I laid down, stared at the ceiling, and said, "Yep, looks just like the clouds in the sky to me."

My apprentice told me he was scared of ladders. I said, "Don't worry, they're more afraid of you than you are of them."

A client asked if I'd paint her hallway for exposure. I said, "Lady, I'm a painter, not a nudist."

I once painted a room so fast the homeowner asked if I'd used a roller or roller skates.

My helper complained the paint was "too runny." I told him, "That's what happens when you put it in the microwave."

A guy asked if I could paint his house invisible. I told him, "Sure, but you'll have to pay in visible money."

I quoted a customer for painting his deck. He said it was too high. I said, "That's funny, I thought you wanted the railing painted too."

A homeowner said, "Can you paint my house like new?" I said, "Sure, but it'll still come with the same old mortgage."

My client asked for a discount if she provided the paint. I said, "Lady, if you provide the paint, I'll provide the comedy."

A kid asked me if I liked my job. I said, "It has its ups and downs — mostly on the ladder."

Joe hopes to finish soon...

Chapter 3: Life on the Jobsite

Dust, ladders, and gallons of coffee—sounds like the perfect setup for a few laughs. On with the jokes-

Why do painters always carry tape? To hang up their wet paint sign.

How do painters like their sandwiches? With plenty of rolls.

What's a painter's favorite game? Hide and streak.

Why don't painters like fast food? Because they hate running drips.

Painters are like magicians—they make cracks disappear.

Why did the painter bring a ladder to the bar? Because he heard the drinks were on the house.

My painter friend doesn't like to gossip—he doesn't want to get into tacky situations.

What's a painter's favorite kind of story? A tall tale.

Why did the paintbrush break up with the roller? It felt like it was being brushed aside.

Painters always win arguments—they have the final coat.

Chapter 4: Customers & Contractors

Sometimes the real comedy is in the conversations with clients. On with more jokes-

Why do customers love painters? Because they always finish with a good impression.

My customer asked if I could paint the house for free—I said, "Sure, but it'll be a shade lighter."

What's a painter's least favorite question? "Can you do it cheaper?"

Why was the painter so trustworthy? Because he always kept things above baseboard.

A painter told his client he'd finish tomorrow… it was a brush with honesty.

What do customers and paint cans have in common? They're both hard to open.

Why don't painters argue with clients? Because they don't want things to get messy.

A customer asked me to make their house look bigger… so, I gave them a smaller brush.

Painters don't lie to customers—they just gloss over the truth.

What's a painter's favorite compliment? "You nailed the first coat!"

Chapter 5: Tool Troubles

I bought a new roller cover. It was so fluffy, I felt like I was painting with a sheep.

My brush fell into the paint bucket. I told the homeowner, "Well, that's one way to get a solid coat."

My sprayer clogged mid-job. The client said, "Is that supposed to happen?" I said, "Yes, it's a built-in coffee break feature."

I once used duct tape instead of painter's tape. Let's just say the walls came out with some "extra texture."

My helper used a broom to roll paint on the ceiling. I said, "Buddy, you're sweeping your career under the rug."

My ladder broke on a job. The homeowner asked, "Do you need to call someone?" I said, "Yeah — a carpenter or a chiropractor."

My brush kept shedding bristles. The client said, "That's a bad brush." I said, "Nope, just balding early."

I spilled paint on my shoes. Now I've got the fanciest "designer work boots" in town.

A roller fell out of my truck and rolled down the street. I yelled, "Don't worry, it's just trying to cover some ground."

I told my apprentice to stir the paint slowly. He brought out a spoon and asked if clockwise or counterclockwise mattered.

Onna loves everything about painting... except watching it dry.

Chapter 6: Tools of the Trade

Brushes, rollers, ladders, and tape—they all have their quirks. On with the jokes-

> Why did the paintbrush go to therapy? It had too many bristles with anxiety.

> What's a roller's favorite type of music? Rock n' roller.

> The ladder asked the roller for help—but the roller said, "Sorry, I'm tied up."

> What's a painter's favorite drink? A coat-tail.

> Why did the painter hug his ladder? It made him feel a little elevated.

> Why do painters love tape? Because it always sticks by them.

> Brushes don't like arguments—they get bent out of shape.

> What's a painter's favorite kind of shoes? Slip-ons.

My brush told me it was tired—I said, "You need a bristle break."

The roller went to the gym… it wanted to get more coverage.

Myles, already climbing the ladder to painter success

Chapter 7: Customers Jokes

A customer asked if I guaranteed my work. I said, "Yes — guaranteed to be painted."

I had a client who wanted "eggshell white" but got mad when it didn't look like an actual egg.

One customer said he wanted his walls "to pop." So, I painted them red and bought him balloons.

A homeowner asked, "How long will the paint last?" I said, "Until your kids discover crayons."

A client wanted to watch me paint. I said, "Sure, but it's only slightly more exciting than watching grass grow."

A lady asked me to paint her bathroom lavender. After I finished, she said, "I meant lavender the flower, not the color."

I painted a guy's living room. He said it looked smaller. I said, "That's called 'cozy.'"

A customer wanted to pay me in cookies. I said, "Depends — are they chocolate chip or oatmeal raisin?"

I had a homeowner complain that the paint smelled. I said, "That's just the aroma of hard work."

A customer asked if I could paint his garage while he was at work. I said, "Sure — but I charge extra for surprise parties."

Chapter 8: Color Me Funny

Every shade tells a story—and sometimes, a joke. On with more jokes-

Why did the red paint get in trouble? It was caught in a shady deal.

Painters love blue—it keeps them from feeling green.

Why did the yellow paint feel left out? Because it wasn't very bold.

Orange you glad I didn't say primer?

Black paint is mysterious—it keeps things under cover.

Green paint is very balanced—it always blends in.

Purple paint is royal—it's always in command.

Beige is boring—but it still gets the job done.

My client asked for grey—I told them that was a concrete idea.

What's a painter's favorite holiday? Color-ween.

Chapter 9: Classic Painter Life

I painted a room twice by mistake. The customer thought I was "just being thorough."

My truck smells like paint. My wife says it's my "signature cologne."

I showed up to a job with paint already on my clothes. The client said, "Looks like you've been here before."

I took a day off. My roller filed a complaint for abandonment.

My phone autocorrected "coat" to "goat." Now I've got a reputation as the "goat painter."

I've painted so many trim lines that I see straight edges in my sleep.

The paint store clerk asked if I wanted a gallon or five. I said, "Yes."

My wife asked why my hair is always stiff. I said, "It's just the lacquer holding me together."

I've been painting so long that even my coffee mug has a fresh coat on it.

I told a client I needed to take a break. He asked if I'd "hit a wall."

Jeff's advice:
Don't look down.

Chapter 10: Workers & Helpers

My apprentice painted himself into a corner. I told him, "Congratulations, you're officially part of the union."

I asked my helper to cut in the ceiling. He brought scissors.

My crew showed up late. They said they were "just drying." I said, "That's my line."

One of my guys asked if we had Wi-Fi on the job. I said, "Nope, but we've got lots of paint fumes — they'll take you places."

I had a helper who painted the wrong house. The good news is, the neighbors loved it.

My student painter said he could finish a room inside of 10 minutes. He forgot to mention it would look like modern art when it was finished.

I told my apprentice to prime the wall. He shouted, "You're the prime boss!"

My worker asked if he could go home early. I said, "Sure — just as soon as the walls dry by themselves."

I had a new guy who thought "drop cloth" meant a place to nap.

My helper tried to carry six gallons of paint at once. He ended up starting a new Jackson Pollock on the driveway.

Shawn's technique has one weakness—his eyesight.

Chapter 11: The Contractor's Life

Early mornings, long days, and plenty of laughs to keep the brush moving. On with more jokes-

Why don't painters work for free? Because exposure doesn't pay the bills.

Painters don't retire—they just start to fade.

Why did the painter bring coffee to the job? To stay grounded.

Why don't painters argue about money? Because they know it's all about the bottom coat.

What's a painter's retirement plan? A brush with destiny.

Painters don't get sick—they just feel a little off-color.

My painter buddy tried to quit—but he couldn't brush it off.

Why are painters always happy? Because they brighten everyone's day.

Painting contractors don't like traffic—it messes with their finish times.

Why do painters love Fridays? Time to brush off the week.

Chapter 12: Jobsite Weather Report

Rain delays, sunburns, and the occasional paint freeze... nature has jokes too. On with more jokes-

Why did the painter bring an umbrella? In case of a paint shower.

Painters don't take breaks—they just dry off.

Why was the painter always broke? Too many overhead costs. That's so true, it's funny.

Painting in the rain is tough... it really dampens the mood.

What's a painter's favorite weather? Overcast.

The job went so smoothly, it was like watching paint dry—but in a good way.

Why do painters love summer? More exterior coverage.

Painters don't get bored—they just switch coats.

Why did the painter love winter? No bugs in the paint.

My boss said I should work faster—I told him I was already at full gloss.

Chapter 13: Quick Punchlines

I painted my shed last weekend. Now the lawn mower refuses to go inside — says it's too fancy.

I used leftover paint for my garage. Now the garage matches a stranger's bathroom.

I painted a door shut once. Best security system ever.

My buddy painted his truck. Now no one can find it because it blends in with houses.

I painted a ceiling fan. Now it looks like a helicopter.

My kid spilled juice on the wall. I told him, "Good choice of accent color."

I painted a client's office gray. He said it felt depressing. I told him, "Perfect for Monday mornings."

I painted my toolbox yellow. Now I can't tell the difference between tools and bananas.

I painted a bathroom mint green. The homeowner said it felt "refreshing." I said, "That's the toothpaste talking."

I painted my shoes white once. Now everyone thinks I'm a pro tennis player.

Chapter 14: Painting Puns & Wordplay

Painters have the best wordplay—smooth, glossy, and full of coverage. On with more jokes-

I'm friends with all my colors—we're on the same palette.

What's a painter's favorite TV show? "Coat of Thrones."

Why did the painter love Shakespeare? Because he liked dramatic strokes.

My painting jokes are terrible—but at least they have good coverage.

Why did the paint roller quit? It was tired of going in circles.

Painters are never late—they're always brushed up.

A painter's diet? Low-drip, high-finish.

My favorite color is green—because it really grows on you.

What's a painter's favorite car? A coat-mobile.

I told my painter buddy to lighten up... so he added more white.

Chapter 15: More Ridiculous Situations

A customer asked if I'd paint her house like the Sistine Chapel. I told her, "Only if you provide Michelangelo."

I painted my neighbor's shed as a surprise. Turns out he wanted it left rusty.

I painted a guy's fence. He said it looked shorter. I told him, "Paint has shrinking powers."

I dropped a roller off a ladder once. It painted a perfect stripe down my pants.

My helper asked what "satin finish" meant. I told him it was paint blessed by monks.

I painted an accent wall red. The client said it made her hungry. I said, "You're welcome."

I left a brush in the paint overnight. It turned into modern sculpture.

My apprentice painted over the light switches. I told him, "Congratulations, you invented touch-sensitive paint."

A client asked if I'd paint her doghouse. The dog said, "Make it bone white."

I painted a deck once and the squirrels walked across it. Now they have matching socks.

Chapter 16: Quick One-Liners

Perfect for jobsite banter, coffee breaks, or your next social media post. On with the jokes-

Painting contractors are good at cover-ups.

Painters: bringing color to your life, one coat at a time.

A painter's work is never finished—it's just well-coated.

Painters never get bored—they just add another layer.

A painting job is like a sandwich—best with multiple layers.

Painters don't cut corners—they cut in.

Every painter dreams in full gloss.

Painters are the masters of smooth finishes.

What's a painter's motto? Just roll with it.

Painters don't spill secrets—they spill paint.

Nicole really enjoys working on high ladders.

Chapter 17: Silly Endings

My buddy asked if I could paint camouflage. I said, "Sure, but you won't be able to find it afterward."

A guy wanted glow-in-the-dark paint. Now his bedroom looks like a rave.

I painted a shed blue. The neighbor painted his green. Now the yards look like a sports rivalry.

My helper painted the outlet covers. Now plugging in the toaster is a mystery adventure.

I painted a client's mailbox. The mailman said, "Finally, something worth delivering to."

My kid painted the dog by mistake. Now he's the neighborhood mascot.

I painted my garage floor. Now my car slips in like it's on ice.

A customer said the color wasn't what she expected. I said, "Neither was your check."

My wife asked if I could paint the kitchen. I told her I was on a break. That was three years ago.

I once painted a bathroom so small I had to step outside to turn around.

Chapter 18: Closing Coat of Laughs

The final coat makes all the difference—so let's finish strong. On with the jokes-

I tried stand-up comedy as a painter… but my jokes didn't stick.

Painters never get lonely—they always have brushes with greatness.

The hardest part of painting? Keeping a straight face while cutting in.

Painters don't do drama—they just add color.

My painter friend said he'd quit tomorrow… but that was just a second coat of excuses.

Painters don't gossip—they gloss over details.

Why was the painter always confident? Because he had strokes of genius.

What do painters do on vacation? Brush up on relaxation.

The life of a painter? Full of ups and downs... mostly on ladders.

Painters never fade—they just keep on rolling.

Funny... that color
looks better on you..."

Chapter 19: A Final 20 Quick Laughs

My apprentice painted the ladder. Now we've got a permanent accent piece.

I spilled paint on the driveway. My neighbor said it added curb appeal.

I painted the wrong side of a fence once. The neighbor was thrilled.

I painted my lunchbox by accident. Now I can't tell it from the toolbox.

A guy asked if I did touch-ups. I said, "Only if the wall apologizes first."

I painted my garage red. Now the bulls in town keep charging it.

My helper painted himself into a closet. We haven't seen him since.

I painted my shed yellow. Now bees won't leave me alone.

I painted my living room black. My wife said it felt like a cave. I said, "Good, Batman's moving in."

A client asked if I offered eco-friendly paint. I said, "Yes, it's green."

I painted the porch steps. Then I slipped down them. At least it was a smooth finish.

My helper dropped a gallon of paint. Now the driveway is "marble style."

I painted the bathroom ceiling blue. The homeowner asked if it came with seagulls.

A guy wanted his house painted fast. I told him, "Great, I'll use watercolors."

I painted a door purple. The homeowner said, "Looks like royalty lives here." I said, "Yeah, Prince."

My truck has so much paint inside, I call it "The Color Mobile."

I painted the window shut once. The homeowner thanked me for lowering his heating bill.

My apprentice mixed all the leftover paints together. Now we own the patent for "Ugly Beige."

I painted my own bedroom gray. My wife said it perfectly matches my personality.

I once painted a wall so straight, the homeowner asked if I used a laser. I said, "Nope, just coffee."

"I put "fore" in performance.

Funny Painter Stories -
The Pizza, the Dog and the
Painter

Jeff the house painter had one weakness: pizza. He
could resist drips, clients who wanted "just one
more coat," and even the temptation to paint
everything "Antique White," but when it came to
pizza—forget it.

One scorching afternoon, halfway through painting
Mrs. Henderson's kitchen, he ordered an extra-
large pepperoni with extra cheese. He was about to
dive in when *Pepper the dog*—Mrs. Henderson's
lumbering golden retriever—loped into the room.
Josh was no ordinary dog. He was part canine, part
vacuum cleaner, and part criminal mastermind.
Jeff sat on a stool, balancing a slice of pizza in one
hand and his roller in the other. He blinked once,
and the pizza vanished.

"Hey!" Jeff shouted, staring at his empty hand.
Pepper sat in the corner, tail wagging, cheese
stretching from his mouth like mozzarella confetti.
"Pepper!" Mrs. Henderson scolded from the other
room. "You leave that nice painter alone!"

Jeff tried to protect the rest of the box. He put it on the counter, out of reach. But Pepper was patient. Like a furry ninja, he waited until Jeff climbed the ladder. Then—*wham!*—Josh leapt, grabbed the whole pizza box, and sprinted across the room. In the chaos, Pepper ran straight through a tray of wet paint. His paws left perfect white paw prints across the hardwood, the carpet, and finally, the pizza box itself.

By the time Jeff caught him, Pepper was proudly sitting in the middle of the living room with his paw on the box, looking like Picasso with a pepperoni.

"Mrs. Henderson," Jeff called out, "your dog just ate my lunch AND decorated your floor."
Mrs. Henderson peeked in, saw the white paw prints, and gasped. "Oh no! My floors!"
Jeff sighed. "Well, good news is, Pepper has an eye for design. Bad news is, I'm still hungry."
Pepper burped loudly. A piece of pepperoni slid out onto the drop cloth.

Jeff bent down, picked it up, and said, "You know what? I think I just invented *Dog-Style Deep Dish.*"

From then on, every time Jeff painted for Mrs. Henderson, Pepper got his own pizza. It was the only way to keep the paint job paw-print free.

Funny Painter Stories -
The Painter and the Widow

Mrs. Daniels had been widowed so long that even her TV remote gave her the silent treatment. Her roses were her only friends—though, to be fair, she insisted they whispered compliments back.

One Tuesday, she decided her house looked less "quaint country charm" and more "abandoned barn in a horror movie." She called Patrick the painter, who was cheaper than therapy and came with unlimited bad jokes.

Patrick showed up in paint-splattered overalls, balancing a ladder on one shoulder and a bucket on the other. He looked like a circus act waiting for applause.

"Good morning, Mrs. Daniels!" he shouted, as though she was hard of hearing. (She wasn't.)

"I'm here to slap some color on these walls and maybe some cheer in your heart!"

Mrs. Daniels squinted at him. "Do you always talk like a motivational poster?" Patrick winked. "Only when I'm being paid by the hour."

He set up his ladder, climbed two steps, then yelled down:

"Hey, do you know why painters always have clean jokes?"

"Why?" she sighed.

"Because dirty ones would leave streaks!"

Mrs. Daniels nearly spit her lemonade.
As Patrick painted, he kept narrating like he was on a cooking show.

"Ah yes, here we apply a generous coat of 'Creamy Almond,' which pairs beautifully with *day-old coffee* and *existential dread.*"

At one point, Mrs. Daniels peeked out the window.

"Patrick, are you talking to the siding?"

"Of course. Houses get lonely too, you know. Look at these cracks—they're practically begging for conversation." By noon, Mrs. Daniels was laughing so hard her neighbors called to ask if she was having a party. "Yes," she replied, "just me, a painter, and a gallon of questionable primer."

When Patrick finished, the house gleamed like a Hallmark movie set. He packed up his brushes dramatically, like a magician bowing after the big trick.

"Well, Mrs. Daniels," he said, "your house is smiling again."

She patted his arm. "So am I, Patrick. You may charge for painting, but the laughter? That's priceless."

Patrick winked. "Don't worry—I threw that in as a free second coat."

As he drove away, Mrs. Daniels finally realized she didn't feel like a lonely widow anymore. She felt like the proud owner of the town's brightest house… and the best comedy show on her front lawn.

Funny Painter Stories -The Basement, a Painter and a Leather Chair

Mike the painter got called in for a basement renovation job. Mrs. Carmichael had just finished turning her dark, musty cellar into a "modern lounge," complete with a pool table, a wet bar, and—her pride and joy—a shiny new leather recliner.

"Mike," she said, patting the chair like it was a family pet, "I don't care what happens to this basement. Just don't get paint on *my chair*. It was imported from Italy."

Mike puffed up his chest. "Ma'am, I've been painting 20 years. Not a drop has *ever* landed where it didn't belong."

Famous last words.

Mike started cutting in around the ceiling while the radio blasted. Everything was going fine until he backed up his ladder—right into the leather chair. The wet brush he was holding? It swung like a sword and left a perfect, three-foot-long white stripe across the armrest.

Mike froze.

He panicked, grabbed a rag, and started scrubbing. Big mistake. The paint smeared until the chair looked less like Italian luxury and more like a Holstein cow.

"Think, Mike, think!" he muttered. His eyes darted to the renovation supplies: duct tape, a throw blanket, and a stack of decorative pillows. With the reflexes of a man covering a crime scene, he draped the blanket over the chair and piled the pillows high.

Minutes later, Mrs. Carmichael walked in. "Mike, how's it—oh! Look at you, decorating already!"

"Yep," Mike said, sweating through his coveralls. "I call it... *Tuscan farmhouse chic.*" She smiled. "Wonderful! I knew you had an eye for design."

Just then, her dog leapt onto the chair, knocking the pillows to the floor. The white-streaked leather shone like a neon sign.

Mrs. Carmichael screamed. Mike blurted the only thing he could think of:

"Good news—it comes with a custom paint finish! Absolutely free!"

Funny Painter Stories -The Painter, the Realtor, and the Patio Lanterns

George the painting contractor was hired by Linda, a high-energy real estate agent who talked faster than an auctioneer. Her latest listing was a "cozy fixer-upper"—which, in realtor-speak, meant the house looked like it had been attacked by raccoons and a lawnmower at the same time.

"George, darling, I need this house to *pop!* Buyers need to feel like they've walked into their dream home, not a tax write-off," Linda said, waving her clipboard like a magic wand.

George nodded. "Fresh paint always helps."
He set up ladders and tarps while Linda zoomed around staging fake fruit bowls and strategically placing candles. Everything was going smoothly—until George stumbled across a dusty cardboard box shoved in a corner of the garage. The label read: *Patio Lanterns – Do Not Throw Out.*

Curiosity got the better of him. He opened the box and found twenty tangled strings of old patio lanterns—plastic globes shaped like pineapples, flamingos, and, for some reason, Elvis heads.

"Perfect!" Linda squealed when she saw them. "We'll string them up in the backyard for ambiance!"

George was skeptical. "Linda, they look like they were last used at a barbecue in 1978."
"Nonsense," she snapped. "They scream retro charm!"

So George reluctantly helped hang the lanterns along the back deck while Linda fluffed pillows inside. But when he plugged them in, the lights didn't just flicker—they *exploded* into a psychedelic strobe show, flashing like a disco on fast-forward.

The timing couldn't have been worse. At that exact moment, Linda arrived with a family of potential buyers.

"Here's the backyard oasis!" she announced proudly, flinging open the patio doors.
The family stepped out and were immediately assaulted by a blinding neon nightmare of flamingos and Elvis heads pulsing like they were at a Vegas rave.

The buyers' little boy screamed with delight.
"COOLEST HOUSE EVER!" he yelled, breakdancing on the deck.

George panicked, tripped over an extension cord, and knocked over a bucket of paint, which splattered all over the deck—and several of the lanterns. Now Elvis had white hair, the flamingos looked like swans, and the pineapples resembled bowling balls.

Linda froze, then turned to the buyers with her best professional smile.

"See? One-of-a-kind property. Comes with… uh… customizable patio lighting!"

The dad nodded thoughtfully. "You know what? We'll take it."

George stared in disbelief. The disco lantern disaster had *sold the house.*

Linda beamed. "George, darling, you're not just a painter—you're a *marketing genius.*"

George sighed. "Great. Do I get paid extra in patio lanterns or what?"

About the Author

Jeff Lockwood is a highly successful businessman and internationally recognized expert in the painting industry. Over the course of his career, he has built a nearly seven-figure painting company from the ground up, earning a reputation for his sharp business acumen, practical strategies, and results-driven approach.

As the author of many published books, Jeff has become a trusted voice for entrepreneurs and tradespeople around the world. His works cover a wide range of topics, from estimating behind a profitable business to marketing, sales, and leadership skills that help business owners thrive.

Jeff's insights have reached readers across North America and beyond, and his expertise has been featured at major industry events, on radio, and in print. Whether through his books, speaking engagements, or one-on-one coaching, Jeff's mission is simple: to inspire, educate, and equip others to achieve their own version of success

"Paint Smart, not Hard" is available on Amazon.

This bestseller offers an in-depth guide to starting and succeeding in the painting business, packed with expert insights, real-life challenges, and practical solutions. With essential knowledge to help you master the residential painting industry, this book is ideal whether you're just beginning or looking to sharpen your business skills.

Available in paperback and Kindle on Amazon, with an audiobook version coming soon.

Don't miss the chance to unlock the secrets to building a thriving residential painting business.

Grab your copy today and start transforming your company.

PUT A COACH IN YOUR CORNER

Looking back, over the years now, when I started out on my own, I wished he would have a painting mentor or a painting business coach to answer questions about the business side of things. I'm sure, if I had someone to consult with occasionally, they would have saved me from spending thousands of dollars in bad marketing choices, buying useless painting equipment and making poor client decisions. So, here I am offering my one-on-one painting business coaching services to you through:

https://www.paintingbizcoach.com

Visit my website and subscribe today.

WATCH JEFF LOCKWOOD ON

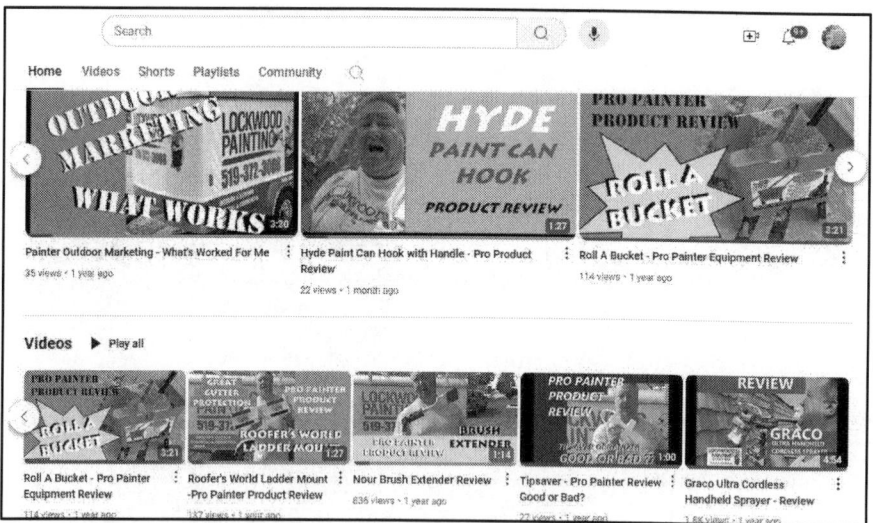

Painting Business Tips, Painter Product Reviews,
Q&A Videos and More.

Check them out at –
https://www.youtube.com/@lockwoodpainting

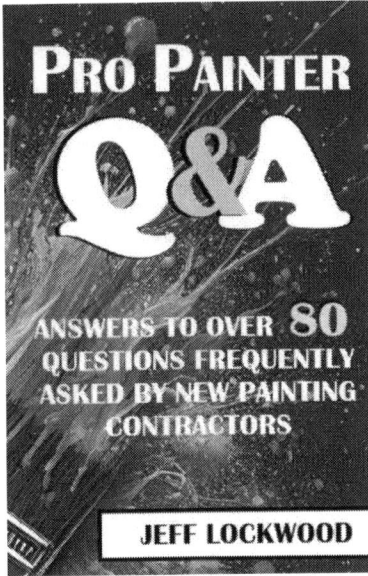

Pro Painter Q&A is your go-to guide for navigating the residential painting industry with confidence. Organized in an easy-to-read Q&A format, it offers practical solutions to the key challenges of running a successful painting business. Covering essential topics like:

- **The Business of Painting**: Actionable insights on operations and financial management.
- **Marketing**: Proven strategies for attracting clients and growing your brand.
- **Sales**: Techniques for closing more deals and presenting compelling proposals.
- **Customer Service**: Tips for building lasting relationships and securing referrals.
- **Estimating**: Step-by-step guidance for accurate and profitable quotes.

Packed with straightforward answers and industry expertise, Pro Painter Q&A is an indispensable resource for contractors at any stage of their business journey, helping you thrive in a competitive market

Mastering the Numbers: A Painting Contractor's Guide to Profitable Estimating is the ultimate guide to pricing painting projects with confidence and precision. Packed with practical insights, this book covers everything a painting contractor needs to know to create accurate, profitable estimates. Readers will begin with *The Fundamentals of Estimating*, building a solid foundation for the entire estimating process. Detailed sections on *Materials and Supplies Calculation* provide techniques to measure accurately, select the right products, and avoid over- or under-ordering.

With *Pricing Structures and Strategies*, contractors learn how to set competitive yet profitable rates, adapt pricing models to different types of projects, and utilize value-based pricing to attract premium clients. The book also addresses *Regional Rates and Industry Standards*, equipping readers to adjust their estimates based on local market data and benchmarks. Finally, *Common Estimating Mistakes and How to Avoid Them* helps contractors sidestep costly errors, streamline their workflows, and refine their estimating skills.

This comprehensive guide is designed for painting professionals at any stage of their career, offering the insights and techniques necessary to win more bids, maximize profits, and build a successful painting business

Pro Painter's
MARKETING EDGE

FACEBOOK · HOUSE PAINTER · @ · DIRECT MAIL POSTCARD · Email PAINTING SERVICES · INSTAGRAM · YARD SIGNS · GOOGLE ADS · REFERRAL PROGRAM MARKETING · PAINTER · WORD OF MOUTH · PAINTING · DOOR HANGER

Expert Marketing Strategies to Boost Your Painting Business

ORDER
YOUR COPY
TODAY ON
amazon

SCAN ME

The Painter's Marketing Edge is an essential marketing guide for painting contractors offering practical, targeted strategies to grow your painting business and stand out in a competitive market. Covering topics such as social media marketing, pay-per-click (PPC) advertising, and traditional marketing methods, the book provides actionable tips for crafting effective campaigns that attract clients and increase visibility. Learn how to build a seasonal marketing plan tailored to your peak and slow seasons and discover the power of reputation management through Google and Yelp reviews to boost credibility and attract more leads.

Whether you're new to marketing or looking to refine your approach, this guide delivers the tools you need to drive growth and elevate your painting business.

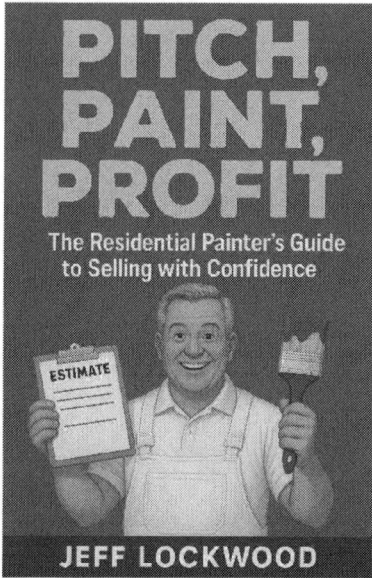

Unlock the Secrets to Closing More Jobs, Without Sounding Like a Salesperson

You've mastered your craft—but closing residential painting jobs still feels like a struggle. **Pitch, Paint, Profit** is your step-by-step guide to selling painting services with confidence and consistency. Learn how to pre-qualify leads, build instant trust during estimates, present your price without flinching, and follow up like a pro. Packed with real-world scripts and proven strategies, this book will help you win better clients, book more jobs, and end the feast-or-famine sales cycle for good.

Stop selling yourself short. Start selling with confidence.

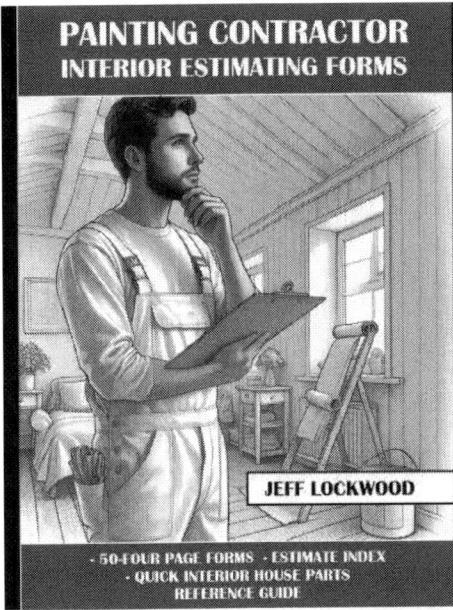

PAINTING CONTRACTOR
INTERIOR ESTIMATING FORMS

JEFF LOCKWOOD

- 50-FOUR PAGE FORMS - ESTIMATE INDEX
- QUICK INTERIOR HOUSE PARTS
  REFERENCE GUIDE

"The Painting Contractor's Interior Estimating Form Book" is a must-have tool for new painting contractors, featuring 50 four-sheet estimate forms in an 8.5 x 11-inch size. Created by an experienced contractor, this form book helps residential painters gather detailed info and estimate interior projects more accurately and efficiently.

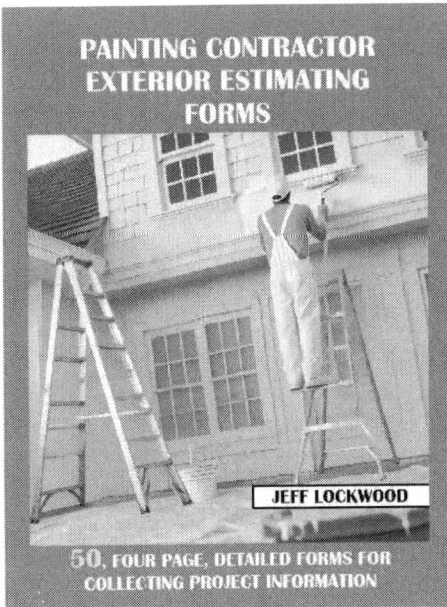

PAINTING CONTRACTOR
EXTERIOR ESTIMATING
FORMS

JEFF LOCKWOOD

50, FOUR PAGE, DETAILED FORMS FOR
COLLECTING PROJECT INFORMATION

"Painting Contractor Exterior Estimating Forms" is a practical tool designed for new painting contractors. This book includes 50 four-sheet estimate forms (8.5 x 11") to help residential painters quickly and accurately estimate exterior painting and staining projects. Designed by an experienced contractor to streamline the process.

Crafting knowledge-packed books tailored exclusively for painting contractors—because your business growth is our mission.

Painting Biz Publishing is a specialized publishing company dedicated to producing high-quality, informative resources tailored specifically for painting contractors and professionals in the painting industry. Our goal is to empower painters, painting business owners, and contractors with the tools, knowledge, and expertise they need to grow and succeed in a competitive market.

All of our book titles are available to purchase from the "Shop" page on our website or on Amazon. Just search for "Jeff Lockwood" when on Amazon.

Printed in Dunstable, United Kingdom